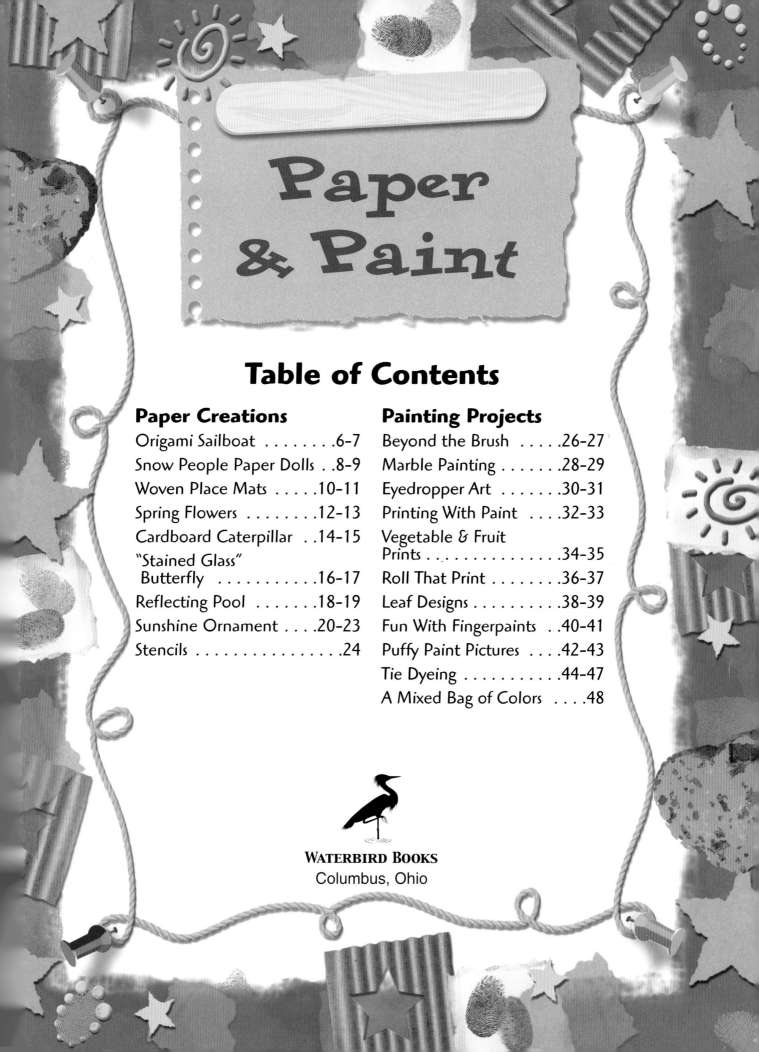

Paper & Paint

Table of Contents

WATERBIRD BOOKS
Columbus, Ohio

President:
Vincent F. Douglas

Publisher:
Tracey E. Dils

Project Editors:
Joanna Callihan,
Lindsay Ann Mizer

Art Director:
Robert Sanford

Interior Design and Production:
Christopher Fowler,
Suzanne Reinhart

 McGraw Hill | Children's Publishing

This edition published in the United States of America in 2003 by Waterbird Books,
an imprint of McGraw-Hill Children's Publishing,
a Division of The McGraw-Hill Companies
8787 Orion Place
Columbus, Ohio 43240-4027

www.MHkids.com

Library of Congress Cataloging-in-Publication Data is on file with the publisher.

Printed in the United States of America.

1-57768-527-X (HC) 0-7696-3152-5(PB)

1 2 3 4 5 6 7 8 9 10 PHXBK 09 08 07 06 05 04 03

The **McGraw-Hill** Companies

Using This Book

- After choosing a craft, check the list marked "What you'll need." These items are the art supplies and tools you will need to make the craft. Some materials are listed as "optional." That means that you can use them, but you do not need them for the craft. You might base your decision on whether you want a certain look or whether that item is readily available.

- The next thing you should do is read all the directions before you start the craft. You should also read the "Suggestion(s)," which might involve different tools or materials.

- Then, collect the materials and follow "Here's how" to make the craft.

Improving Cutting Skills

Some children who are still learning how to use scissors cannot seem to cut on the lines no matter how hard they try. This problem can often be fixed in a fun way. Check to see "who is in the driver's seat"; that is, check for correct finger placement. Correct finger placement involves the use of the thumb and the middle finger, not the index finger. The middle finger has more strength and maintains better control.

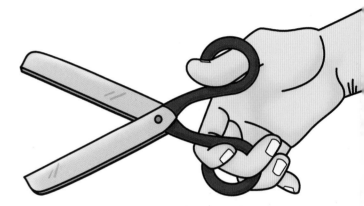

If the opening in the handle is large enough, both the index and middle fingers can be inserted. However, the index finger is only "going along for the ride." The thumb and the middle finger do all the work (driving).

If your child's fingers are too large for the scissors, he/she may need to readjust the grip and eliminate the use of the index finger when cutting.

Be ready to do any cutting for your child as needed. A younger child especially may need supervision. Don't let him/her get discouraged if you need to take over. Continue to provide your child with opportunities to practice cutting.

Painting Tips

Watercolor paints, the kind in a plastic, boxed palette, are used most often in this book. When tempera paint is used, you will find liquid tempera more convenient and easier to measure than the powdered form.

Some activities call for paint dishes. Pie pans or foam trays work well for these activities. However, it is recommended that you use clean foam trays from supermarket-packaged baked goods, fruits, or vegetables, because meat and poultry trays are difficult to disinfect. You can also mix paint in an ice cube tray or muffin tin.

The Color Wheel

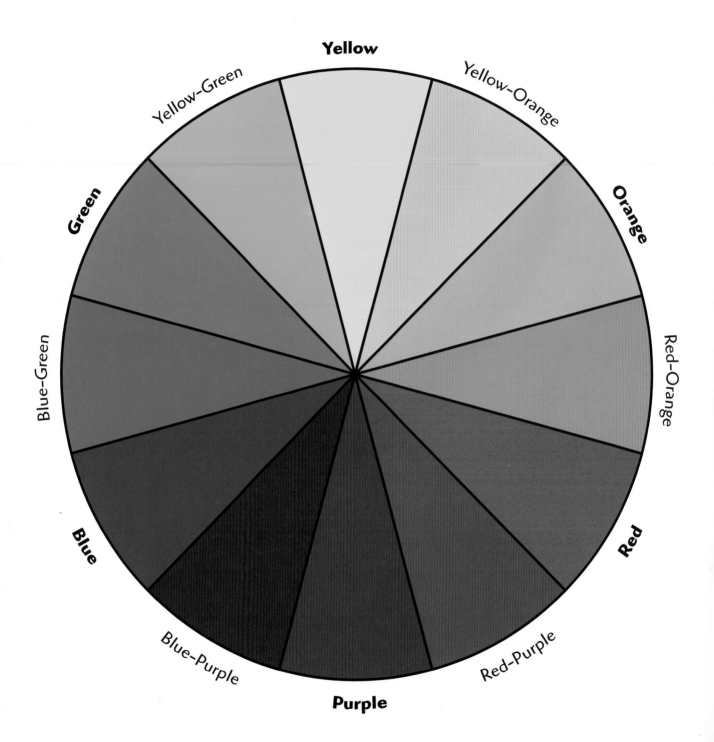

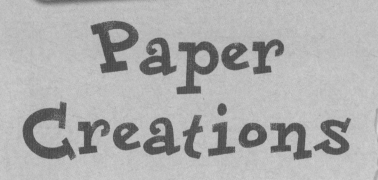

Paper Creations

Paper art can be simple, fun, and very creative. You can tear it, cut it, draw on it, paint it, layer it, color it, crumple it, fold it, or add it to another material. Paper is used to create many forms of art, such as drawing, painting, paper maché, and origami. For example, by using simple folding techniques, you can turn a plain sheet of paper into a three-dimensional sailboat or even a spring flower.

The Paper Creations section uses a variety of paper products and things such as crayons, scissors, and glue. After you turn your simple paper into a rabbit or a beautiful butterfly, you may never look at a sheet of paper the same way again!

Origami Sailboat

Origami is the ancient art of folding paper. Amazing figures can be made without cutting or gluing!

What you'll need

- ☐ white construction paper or any unlined paper
- ☐ crayons or markers
- ☐ scissors

Boy Oh Buoy!

1. Cut the construction paper into a square with 4-inch sides.

2. Fold your paper in half diagonally, then fold it in half diagonally again.

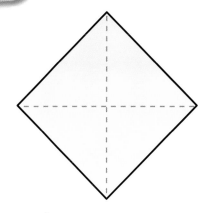

3. Unfold the paper once to make a triangle.

4. Fold one edge up to meet the halfway line (see diagram on the right).

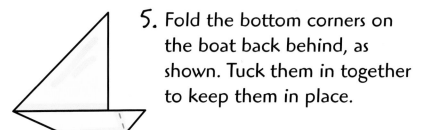

5. Fold the bottom corners on the boat back behind, as shown. Tuck them in together to keep them in place.

6. Decorate your sail with crayons or markers and write the boat's name on one side.

Boy Oh Buoy!

Snow People Paper Dolls

Make an entire family of snow people just by folding and cutting! Use colored paper, markers, and glitter to decorate them.

What you'll need

- rectangular white paper (18" x 24" works best)
- markers or crayons
- pencil
- scissors
- glue (optional)
- scraps of colored construction paper (optional)

Here's how . . .

1. Make an accordion fold with the white paper as shown. When folded, the width of the paper should be about 3 or 4 inches across. (The number of folds depends on your paper size.)

2. Use a pencil to draw a snow person outline that goes a little bit off the paper, as shown. You may want an adult to draw it for you.

3. Cut out the snow person, cutting through all the layers of paper at once. Do not cut off the entire fold.

4. Unfold your paper and draw clothes and faces for each figure. Cut out hat and scarf shapes from the colored construction paper and glue them onto the snow people.

Suggestion

● You can create other figures, such as angels or children holding hands.

Woven Place Mats

Weaving your own place mats is easy and fun—and they make mealtime special for your family!

What you'll need

- [ ] 12" x 18" construction paper in 2 different-colored sheets
- [ ] ruler
- [ ] pencil
- [ ] scissors
- [ ] glue

1. Take one sheet of construction paper and draw a line 1 inch from the top. Fold the construction paper in half, as shown.

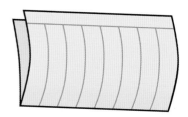

2. Draw lines about 1 1/2 inches apart from the top line to the fold, as shown.

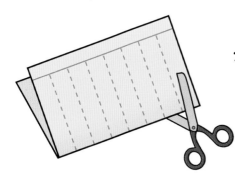

3. Cut on the lines from the fold to the line.

4. Cut the second piece of construction paper into 1 1/2 inch strips across the width of the paper, as shown.

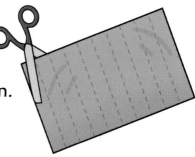

5. Use these strips to weave through the strips of the first sheet of construction paper. To weave means to take the strip under the paper, then take it over the paper at the next opening.

6. When you have finished weaving the entire mat, glue the ends of the strips down on the back side.

Suggestion

● Draw and cut wavy instead of straight lines (steps 2 and 3) for a more fun look.

Spring Flowers

Brighten someone's day! Make several flowers for a paper bouquet.

What you'll need

- ☐ construction paper, green and other colors
- ☐ crayons or markers
- ☐ scissors
- ☐ glue
- ☐ paper hole punch (optional)

Here's how . . .

1. Cut a circle about 1 1/2 inches across out of construction paper.

2. Glue dots from a hole punch or color a design in the center of the flower.

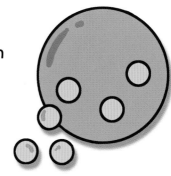

3. Cut out 1/2 inch by 2 1/2 inch strips of construction paper to make petals.

4. Glue the ends of the petals together, as shown.

5. Glue the petals onto the back of the circle, as shown. You may need to hold it for a minute while it dries.

6. Cut a stem and some leaves from the green construction paper and glue them to the flower.

Suggestions

- Glue another ring of petals behind the first set.

- Use longer strips to make longer petals.

Cardboard Caterpillar

You can make wild and wacky or simple and sweet caterpillars using household materials and a little imagination.

What you'll need

- ☐ paper towel or toilet paper cardboard rolls
- ☐ colorful paper of any and all types (tissue paper, wrapping paper, construction paper)
- ☐ pipe cleaner
- ☐ pom-poms, buttons, or cotton balls
- ☐ wiggly eyes
- ☐ glue
- ☐ scissors
- ☐ paper hole punch

1. Cut a strip of paper 1 inch wide. Wrap it around the cardboard roll. Trim off any extra paper.

2. Cut more strips in different colors the same length, using the first strip as your pattern.

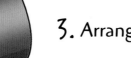

3. Arrange the strips in a pattern.

4. Glue each strip around the cardboard roll.

5. Punch a hole close to one end of the roll. Bend a pipe cleaner in half and stick the middle in the hole. The parts sticking out form the antennae.

6. Place a pom-pom sticking out of the same end.

7. Glue wiggly eyes on the pom-pom.

Suggestion

- Use other small decorations to create your own Cardboard Creature.

"Stained Glass" Butterfly

Look! Is that a butterfly in your house? Your friends will think so when they see your colorful see-through butterfly!

1. Fold the black paper in half lengthwise.

2. Draw half an outline of a butterfly.

3. Repeat the outline 1 inch inside the first outline, as shown. Leave space between the outlines.

4. With the design still folded in half, cut out the outline and inside of the shapes. Leave the borders uncut.

5. Unfold the butterfly and cut tissue paper to cover each opening. Make the tissue paper slightly larger than the opening.

6. Glue the tissue paper to the back of the butterfly, covering each opening.

7. Punch a hole near the top and tie on a string.

8. Hang the butterfly from the ceiling or in a window.

Suggestions

● Try your own wing design.

● If you hang your butterfly, you may want to glue another black construction paper frame onto the back so it looks nice from both sides.

Reflecting Pool

Use this easy trick to make a masterpiece. One turn of your paper and you've created a beautiful reflecting pool!

What you'll need

- ☐ white paper
- ☐ pencil
- ☐ crayons
- ☐ watercolor or watered-down tempera paint
- ☐ paintbrush

1. Use a pencil to draw a horizon line separating the sky from the water across your paper.

2. Draw scenery above your horizon line. Possible choices include mountains, sun, land, trees, or boats.

3. Turn the paper upside down.

4. Repeat the drawing to create the reflection, using wavy lines across the paper to imitate the movement of the water.

5. Turn the drawing to its first position.

6. With crayons, color the parts identically that are above and below the horizon line.

7. Paint over the entire surface below the horizon line with a coat of blue paint. Use wavy strokes for water movement.

Sunshine Ornament

Use pieces of crayon to make . . . a window ornament? You won't believe how bright it will look.

What you'll need

- [ ] two 9" paper plates
- [ ] crayons in shades of yellow, red, and orange
- [ ] wax paper
- [ ] yellow, red, or orange construction paper
- [ ] an iron and ironing board
- [ ] paper towels
- [ ] cheese or vegetable grater
- [ ] yarn, string, or thread for hanging
- [ ] white glue
- [ ] scissors
- [ ] pencil
- [ ] an adult

1. Carefully cut out the centers from the paper plates, leaving the rims uncut.

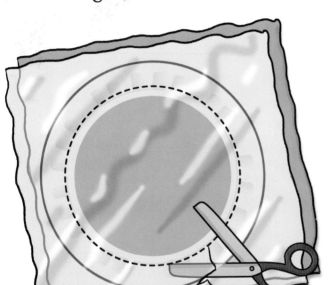

2. Cut 2 sheets of wax paper slightly larger than the hole in the plate.

3. Draw and cut out a circle from the construction paper. Make it smaller than a soda pop can. This is the middle of your sun.

4. Protect your ironing board with several layers of paper towels. Place one wax paper circle on the towels and place your cut out construction paper drawing on top of the wax paper.

5. Remove the labels from your crayons. Have an adult use a grater to shave small chips off each crayon so they fall around the paper cut out. You need only a few chips of each color. These will become the sun's rays.

(continued on next page)

6. Carefully cover the picture with the other wax paper circle. Add another layer of paper towels on top of the wax paper.

7. Have an adult press the two wax paper circles together with a warm iron until the crayon chips are melted.

8. Apply glue around the inside rim of one plate and place your pressed wax paper picture inside the glued rim.

9. Place one end of a long piece of yarn above the picture to be the hanger.

10. Place the other plate rim inside the glued rim containing the picture ornament. Make sure the yarn is between the plates.

11. When the glue is dry, hang your ornament in a window.

Suggestion

● Create these other variations below or make up your own!

Stencils

Cut stencils in the shapes of letters, numbers, patterns, or symbols. Fill them in with crayons, markers, or paint to create cards, make patterns, or just to practice writing.

Here's how . . .

1. Draw shapes, numbers, or letters with a pen on the plastic lids.

2. Have an adult use sharp scissors to poke through each lid within the design and begin cutting out the shape.

3. Finish cutting out the shape or have an adult cut it out for you.

4. Trace the shapes onto white paper.

What you'll need

- ☐ plastic lids from coffee cans or margarine containers
- ☐ white paper
- ☐ scissors
- ☐ pencil
- ☐ pen
- ☐ an adult

Painting Projects

If you can pick up a brush, you can be a painter! Since the beginning of time, people have been using brushes and other objects to swirl colored dyes and paints around in order to communicate and be creative. The first "masterpieces" may have been painted on the walls of ancient caves!

This section shows you how to use "brush substitutes" like cotton swabs, rags, and even marbles! The first painters used natural dyes and berries to create their own paint. You can create your own paint, too, using common items from around the house. Don't forget to prepare your work area before you begin. That means covering the work surface with newspaper; using an old paint shirt to protect your clothes; and having plenty of soap, water, and paper towels on hand for cleanup.

Beyond the Brush

Who says you need a paintbrush to paint? Experiment with these other kinds of "paintbrushes" or come up with some different ones of your own!

Paint With:

Cotton Swabs

You can use swabs to "draw" with the paint, making more detailed pictures than those painted with most kinds of brushes.

Feathers

One way to use feathers is to paint them with a paintbrush, then paint with the feather as a brush while it is still wet.

Rag Painting

Tear a cotton rag into a 2"x 8" strip and knot it in the middle. Hold the knotted piece of cotton rag by both ends. Coat the knot by rolling it in tempera paint. Roll the rag across the paper, making uneven tracks with the paint-soaked knot.

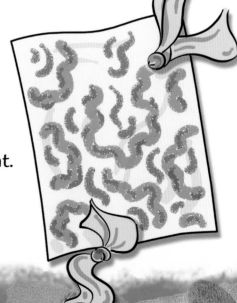

Toy Cars

Dip a toy car in paint to coat the wheels. Then, drive it over the paper to make roads and tracks. When the painting dries, cut out pictures of cars and trucks from toy catalogs or magazines and glue them onto the "road map."

Sponges

Sponges give a very different texture. A kitchen sponge can be used "as is" or cut into a shape to use as a stencil.

Water

A warm, sunny day can inspire you to create designs with water on pavement. Recycle squeeze-type dishwashing liquid bottles for squirting lines and letters on pavement. You can also use wide brushes and sponges.

Marble Painting

You never know what kind of design you'll get when you use marbles to create this project! Roll the marbles and watch the design appear!

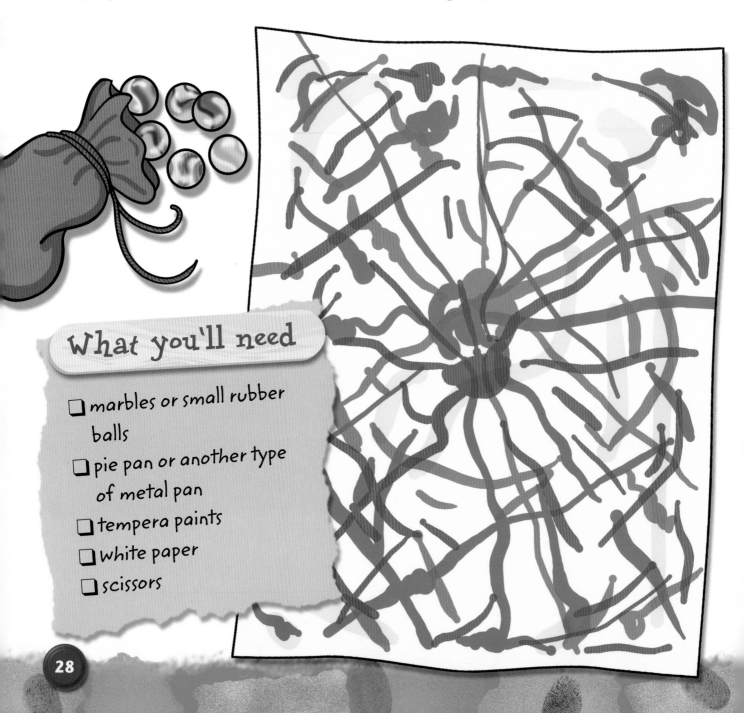

What you'll need

- ❑ marbles or small rubber balls
- ❑ pie pan or another type of metal pan
- ❑ tempera paints
- ❑ white paper
- ❑ scissors

1. Cut paper to fit in the bottom of a pie pan.

2. Squeeze a few drops of paint onto the paper. Then, put a few marbles into the pan. You can use different colors of paint at once or wait until one color dries before adding another color.

3. Hold the pan and gently roll the marbles back and forth through the paint.

Eyedropper Art

What a weird brush! The dropper lets you choose where you want each color to be.

What you'll need

- eyedropper
- food coloring
- paper towels or flattened coffee filters
- construction paper
- muffin tin, ice-cube tray, foam cups, or egg carton
- toothpicks
- water
- glue

1. Fill a tin with water and add a few drops of food coloring to each section. Mix each with a toothpick.

2. Squeeze the rubber end of the eyedropper and dip the other end into a color. Stop squeezing to let the paint fill the dropper.

3. Squeeze the eyedropper to put drops of color on a paper towel.

4. When the paper towel is dry, frame it with construction paper or mount it on a sheet of black construction paper.

Suggestion

- When your design is dry, make a butterfly. Gather the paper towel together in the middle and loop a colorful pipe cleaner around it for the body. Then, twist the pipe cleaner to form antennae.

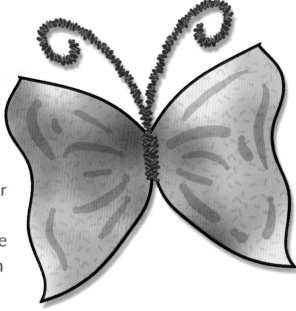

Printing With Paint

Printmaking gives you a way to make a design over and over. There are lots of ways to make prints using paper, blocks, and even leaves!

Paint, Fold, Print!

Fold your paper in half. Then, open it up and paint only on one side of the fold. Fold your paper again and press down on it. When you open the paper, both sides will be printed with the same image.

Alphabet Block Prints

Using wood alphabet blocks with raised letters, dip each block into a pie pan filled with tempera paint. Press the block onto construction paper, then lift it off, straight up. Spell your word in reverse order. Then, hold your paper up to a mirror to decode!

Object Printing

Use any small objects, such as combs, glasses, jar lids, containers, cookie cutters, etc. Dip objects, one at a time, into tempera paint. Press the object onto construction paper, then lift it off, straight up.

Leaf Printing

With the leaf on a baking pan or foam tray, apply an even coat of paint onto the vein-side of the leaf. Paint may be applied with a roller or with brushes. Place a sheet of paper on top of the painted side of the leaf and rub gently with your fingers. Remove the paper and allow time for the paint to dry.

Suggestion

● When done on large paper, any of these prints can be used as wrapping paper.

Vegetable & Fruit Prints

Good food makes great pictures! Let an adult help you do the cutting.

What you'll need

- vegetable or fruit pieces (onions, cabbage, apples, star fruit, mushrooms, etc.)
- tempera paint
- pie pans or aluminum foil
- paper
- knife (for the adult to use)
- butter knife or pencil (optional)
- an adult

1. Have an adult cut each vegetable in half.

2. If desired, use the butter knife to carve out a large outline or picture on the vegetable. Keep it simple.

3. Pour paint into the pie pans.

4. Dip the vegetable or fruit half in the paint. Blot it on scrap paper to even out the paint.

5. Stamp the vegetable half onto the paper gently. Then, lift it straight up.

6. Dip and stamp again to create a design.

7. Continue to stamp, experimenting with placing your stamp in different directions and creating overlapping shapes.

Suggestion

● Have an adult cut the vegetable into different shapes instead of in half.

Roll That Print

Make your own designer paint roller—perfect for making borders or entire pictures!

What you'll need

- [ ] small, sturdy cardboard rolls
- [ ] yarn
- [ ] tempera paint
- [ ] paintbrushes
- [ ] dishes for paint and glue
- [ ] white glue
- [ ] paper
- [ ] scissors

Here's how . . .

1. Cut pieces of yarn 1 to 12 inches long. Then, dip the yarn into a dish of glue.

2. Attach the yarn to the cardboard rolls in patterns and let it dry thoroughly.

3. Once dry, use a paintbrush to paint the yarn.

4. Roll the painted roll on paper to make print designs.

by Matthew

Suggestion

- This makes a perfect border for other art projects.

Leaf Designs

Collect your favorite kinds of leaves. Then, follow the instructions to make your own woods picture.

What you'll need

- ☐ fresh leaves, various shapes and sizes
- ☐ watercolor paints in fall leaf colors
- ☐ paintbrushes
- ☐ pencil
- ☐ black crayon
- ☐ white construction paper

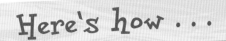

1. With your pencil, trace the outlines of leaves onto white construction paper. Make sure to fill the entire page.

2. Trace over each leaf shape with a thick line of black crayon.

3. Paint the inside of each leaf shape with different fall colors. The black crayon outline will keep the colors from running together.

Suggestions

- Use different color crayons for the leaf outlines.

- Paint the white background area.

Fun With Fingerpaints

Which is more fun—making the picture or looking at it when it's done? With fingerpaints, it's both! Large, glossy fingerpainting paper is best, but you can use other paper or even another smooth, easy-to-clean surface. Here are several different recipes for you to make your own set of paints. With each set, use your fingers to draw and to add texture to your picture.

Flour and Salt Fingerpaint

This fingerpaint has a grainy quality, providing a different sensory experience. Combine 1 cup flour with 1 1/2 teaspoons of salt (or sand). Add 1 cup of water. Food coloring is optional.

Pudding Prints

Fingerpaint using pudding. Then, carefully lay a sheet of paper over your picture, press lightly, and peel back the paper slowly for a copy.

Laundry Detergent Fingerpaint

This type of fingerpaint may be used on a smooth tabletop or on fingerpaint paper. Beat detergent into a small amount of water until you have the consistency of whipped cream. If you are using paper, you can add tempera paint or food coloring and mix it well. Make sure to keep your hands away from your eyes while using this paint.

Textured Fingerpaint

Mix one of the following ingredients into the paint you made: sawdust, coffee grounds, uncooked rice, or flour. To make super slippery paint, add dishwashing liquid or glycerin. For sticky paint that dries with a glossy finish, add corn syrup.

Shaving Cream Fingerpaint

Only a small amount of shaving cream is needed to paint on a non-wood tabletop. It actually cleans the table as you work with it. Since the end product cannot be saved, consider taking photos of the artist at work.

Puffy Paint Pictures

Follow this recipe, and you'll have three-dimensional paint! Wait until it's dry—it's as much fun to touch as it is to see.

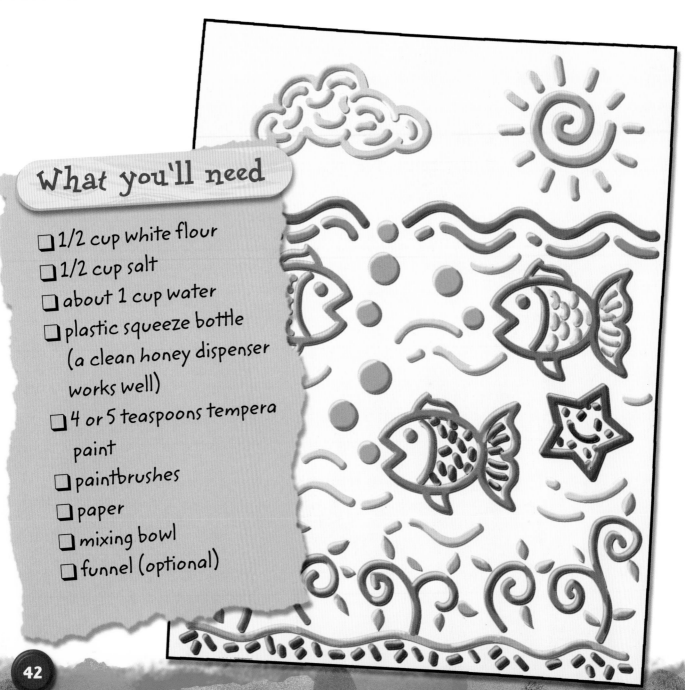

What you'll need

- [ ] 1/2 cup white flour
- [ ] 1/2 cup salt
- [ ] about 1 cup water
- [ ] plastic squeeze bottle (a clean honey dispenser works well)
- [ ] 4 or 5 teaspoons tempera paint
- [ ] paintbrushes
- [ ] paper
- [ ] mixing bowl
- [ ] funnel (optional)

Here's how . . .

1. Stir together the flour, salt, and about half the water in the bowl.

2. Add the tempera paint.

3. Slowly add more water until the mixture can be poured but is not runny.

4. Use the funnel to pour the mixture into a squeeze bottle.

5. Squeeze the paint onto paper. Let the picture dry for several hours.

Suggestion

● Use puffy paint and index cards to make a set of "touchy-feely alphabet cards." They make learning letters fun! You could even use them for a game by putting the letters in a grocery bag and identifying each letter by touch. ("This feels like the letter B.")

Tie Dyeing

Decorate your own clothes with this special project—with your parent's permission!

What you'll need

- a piece of cotton clothing—a tee shirt works well*
- fabric dye**
- buckets or other containers for dye, 1 for each color
- large plastic bag or piece of plastic
- rubber gloves
- rubber bands (optional)
- eyedropper, squeeze bottle, or paintbrush (optional)
- an adult

* Have an adult wash the piece of clothing before doing this project. Do not use fabric softeners or dryer sheets.
** Any kind will do, but make sure to read the label before buying it; some dyes call for extra ingredients.

Here's how . . .

1. Have an adult make the dye, following the directions on the package. Anyone working with the dye throughout the project should wear rubber gloves. Doing the project outside is ideal.

2. Tie off the tee shirt. You can knot sections or bundle up sections and put rubber bands on them. See page 46 for different ways to tie it off. Whichever way you choose, make sure to do it tightly, so that dye stays out of those areas.

3. Have an adult dye your shirt. See page 47 for different ways to dye it. Whichever way you choose, remember that the longer you leave the fabric in the dye, the darker the color will be. Also, the dye will be lighter when dry. To mix colors on your shirt, dye it with a new color. If you want the colors to be more separate, let them dry first.

4. Dry the fabric completely on plastic for 1–3 days.

5. Rinse your project in warm water, one section at a time, then in cool water. Take off the rubber bands (or untie the knots) and rinse the shirt again.

6. Have an adult wash the shirt alone before adding it to the regular laundry.

Suggestions

- Some dyes will set better if you have an adult place the fabric between two sheets of paper and steam it with an iron.

- Tie dye scarves, socks, hats, pillowcases, fabric napkins—anything made with cotton fabric.

Ways to Wrap the Shirt:

Each shirt is its own original project. Each one will be different even if you wrap it the same way!

Regular Tie Dye: ▶
Tie knots in sections of the fabric all over the shirt. Dip different sections into the dye, switching colors as you choose.

◀Sunburst:
Pinch the fabric near the center of the shirt. Lift up and twist it into a tight spiral. Then, roll it into the shape of a donut. Keep it in place with rubber bands. Drip dye on the top, then turn it over and drip dye on top again or dip it into one color.

Star: ▶
Choose five places on the shirt to be the points of your star. Bring the edges of them to the center of the shirt. Put rubber bands around the rest of the "arms." Dye the center using a squeeze bottle or eye dropper. Use a different color on the next sections out from the center. Change colors when you get to the second set of sections from the center, and so on.

Ways to Dye the Shirt:

● Dunk the entire shirt in one color. If you want to change the color, dunk it in another color afterwards.

● Dip sections into a color. Dip sections into different colors if desired. The colors will probably run together depending on how close they are.

● Use an eyedropper or a squeeze bottle to make designs and to keep the colors more separated.

A Mixed Bag of Colors

Try this fun—and non-messy—activity to experiment with mixing your colors!

What you'll need

- ❑ tempera paint
- ❑ 1 cup of powdered laundry detergent
- ❑ resealable plastic bags
- ❑ food coloring
- ❑ mixing bowls
- ❑ water
- ❑ spoon

Here's how . . .

1. Place the laundry detergent in a mixing bowl and add water slowly, while stirring. The mixture should remain thick.

2. Divide the mixture into separate bowls and add a different color to each one.

3. Spoon a small amount of two colors into a plastic bag and seal the bag.

4. Gently rub the soapy mixture together and make the two colors blend together to become a third color.

5. Use a different plastic bag for each color combination you make.